SHARKS!

Written by Janet Palazzo-Craig
Illustrated by Monika Popowitz
Photography by Steve Dolce

Troll

Copyright © 1999 by Troll Communications L.L.C.

Planet Reader is an imprint of Troll Communications L.L.C.

Printed in the United States of America.   ISBN 0-8167-6320-8

10 9 8 7 6 5 4 3

Welcome to Planet Reader!

Invite your child on a journey to a wonderful, imaginative place—
the limitless universe of reading! And there's no better traveling
companion than you, the parent. Every time you and your child read
together you send out an important message: Reading can be
rewarding and *fun*. This understanding is essential to helping your
child build the skills and confidence he or she needs as an emerging
reader.

Here are some tips for sharing Planet Reader stories with your child:

Be open! Some children like to listen to or read the whole story and
then ask questions. Some children will stop on every page with a
question or a comment. Either way is fine; the most important thing
is that your child feels reading is a pleasurable experience.

Be understanding! Sometimes your child might need a direct answer.
If he or she points to a word and asks you to tell what it is, do so.
Other times, your child may want to sound out a word or stop to figure
out a sentence independently. Allow for both approaches.

Enjoy! This book was created especially for your child's age group.
Talk about the story. Take turns reading favorite parts. Look at how
the illustrations support the story and enhance the reading experience.

And most of all, enjoy your child's journey into literacy. It's one of the
most important trips the two of you will ever take!

Shark! What do you think of when you hear that word? Do you imagine sharp teeth flashing? Or do you think of a sleek and deadly hunter swimming through the sea?

tiger shark

Let's look closely at the world of
sharks. Some facts about these
awesome hunters may surprise you.

goblin shark

**leopard
shark**

Did you know there are more than 350 kinds of sharks? Sharks live in all the world's oceans. Some also live in a few of the rivers that lead to the sea.

blue shark

whale shark

Sharks come in many different sizes. The largest is the whale shark. It is also the largest fish in the world! This giant can be more than 50 feet (15 meters) long.

The whale shark is a gentle giant. It eats mostly the tiny sea creatures called *plankton*. When it eats, this shark opens its mouth wide. In goes a huge amount of water, full of tasty plankton! Because the whale shark does not need to chew its food, its teeth are small.

whale
shark

gillrakers

The basking shark is the second largest fish in the world. It also eats plankton. The plankton sticks to special structures in the shark's mouth called *gillrakers*. Gillrakers are like the long bristles of a brush.

basking
shark

The basking shark gets its name
from the way it moves slowly at
the top of the water. It seems to be
basking, or warming itself, in the
sunlight. It's really just busy eating!

lantern
shark

One of the world's smallest sharks
is the lantern shark. It is only 8
inches (20 centimeters) long. That's
small enough to hold in your
hand. The lantern shark gets its
name because it glows in the dark.
This creature makes its home in
some of the deepest, darkest parts
of the ocean.

All sharks are meat-eating fish. But other fish are not the only things a shark will eat. Tin cans, shoes, license plates, and tar paper have all been found in sharks' stomachs! Although some sharks can be dangerous to humans, less than one hundred shark attacks take place each year. Scientists are still trying to find out why sharks sometimes go after people.

mako
shark

The shark's streamlined body, along with its strong, bendable tail and fins, lets the animal move quickly to catch food. Many sharks are well known for their hunting skill. The mako is one of the most ferocious hunters. This swift and powerful swimmer can travel up to 35 miles (56 kilometers) per hour.

The hammerhead is one of the strangest-looking sharks. Do you think its head looks like a hammer? At the ends of the head are the shark's eyes and nostrils. The hammerhead uses its curved, razor-sharp teeth to feed on its favorite food—the stingray.

hammerhead
shark

The angel shark is also unusual.
It has a flat body, and it swims
along the sandy bottom of the sea.
As this shark moves, its extra-long
side fins look like flapping wings.
When a fish swims by, the angel
shark snaps it up.

angel
shark

blue shark

The blue shark
is named for
its blue skin color.
Its large black eyes seem
to stare eerily into the water.
Blue sharks hunt fish, but they
have attacked people, as well.

The most feared shark is the great white. It is named for its white underside. Some of these giants are more than 21 feet (6.4 meters) long.

great white
shark

Imagine the frightening sight
of this powerful swimmer as
it attacks. Its mouth opens.
Two rows of sharp, pointed teeth
close in, tearing into the shark's
unlucky prey. The great white
shark's favorite foods are sea lions,
seals, tuna, and other sharks.

Sharks are fish, but they are different from most fish in several ways. One difference has to do with their skeletons.

Most fish have skeletons made of bone, just as you do. A shark's skeleton is made of a strong, bendable material called *cartilage*. Your ears and the end of your nose are made of cartilage.

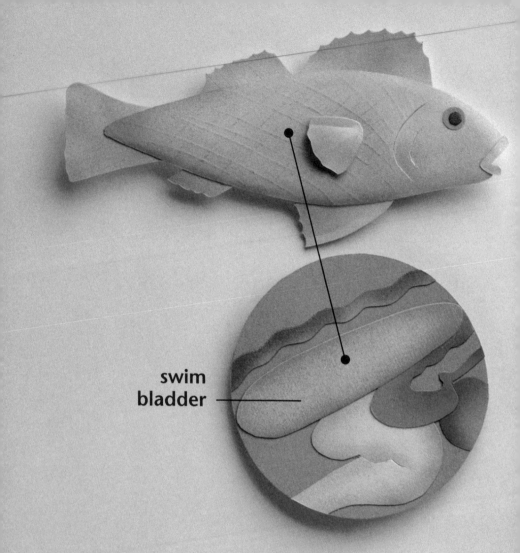

swim
bladder

Another difference is that most
fish have something called a *swim
bladder*. This gas-filled bladder is a
bit like a balloon. It helps keep the
fish from sinking in the water.

Sharks do not have swim bladders. Instead they have large livers filled with oil. Because oil is lighter than water, it helps hold the shark up. Even so, most sharks must keep swimming at all times to stay afloat.

stomach

liver

intestine

Like other fish, sharks breathe by taking in oxygen from the water through their *gills*. Most fish have one pair of gills. Sharks have five to seven pairs of gills.

gill

gills

Most sharks cannot pump water over their gills the way other fish do. These sharks must keep swimming to force water through their mouths and over their gills so they can breathe. One shark that is able to pump water over its gills is the nurse shark. Because it does not need to swim all the time, the nurse shark can rest on the sea bottom. There, it catches lobsters and sea urchins to eat.

nurse shark

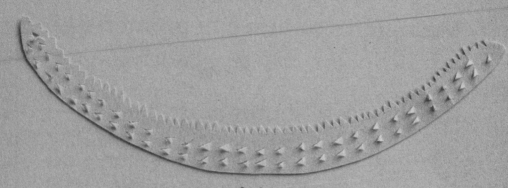
rows of shark teeth

Rows of sharp teeth line the mouths of most sharks. If a tooth falls out, a new one moves in to take its place. The new teeth are bigger than the ones they've replaced.

shark tooth

Sharks' teeth come in
many different shapes
and sizes, depending
on what the shark eats.
Some sharks have teeth
that are like small spikes.
Other sharks have
notched teeth,
for cutting
prey apart.
Sharks with blunt
teeth can easily crush
their food. And sharks
with long, curved,
pointed teeth are great
at grabbing slippery fish.

shark teeth

shark jaw

A shark has keen senses to help it hunt. It can see well in dim light. It can also hear low-pitched sounds very well. Besides having ears inside its head, a shark has something called a *lateral line* along each side of its body.

This line picks up the vibrations made by fish and other prey. By sensing where such movements are, the shark knows where to find its next meal.

lateral line

A shark's sense of smell helps it hunt for food, too. And a shark has special *pores*, or tiny holes, around its nostrils. These pores can sense electrical signals given off by prey.

pores

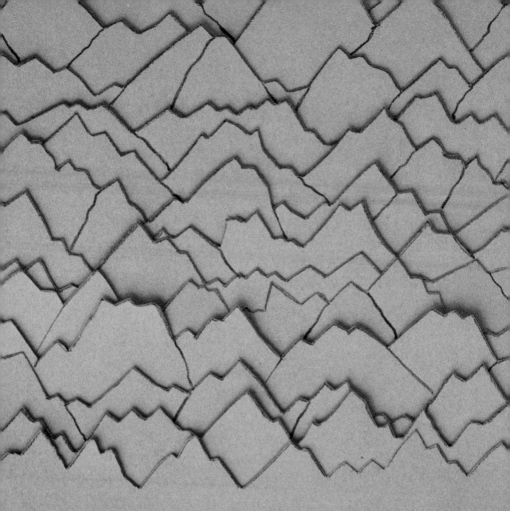

A shark has very different scales on its body than other fish do. A shark's scales, called *sharkskin,* are like small, sharp teeth. Sharkskin is so rough that people use it as sandpaper.

Sharks have been around for almost 400 million years. How do we know this? Scientists find and study ancient shark *fossils*, or remains, such as teeth. The age of these fossils tells us when early sharks lived.

shark fossils

The world of sharks is a fascinating one. If you're ever at an aquarium, you may come face-to-face with a shark. Study it closely—you're sure to have an exciting adventure!

Index